Inside the NFL

THE
TAMPA BAY
BUCCANEERS

BOB ITALIA
ABDO & Daughters

Published by Abdo & Daughters, 4940 Viking Drive, Suite 622, Edina, Minnesota 55435.

Copyright © 1996 by Abdo Consulting Group, Inc., Pentagon Tower, P.O. Box 36036, Minneapolis, Minnesota 55435 USA. International copyrights reserved in all countries. No part of this book may be reproduced in any form without written permission from the publisher.

Printed in the United States.

Cover Photo credit: Wideworld/Allsport
Interior Photo credits: Wide World Photos
Bettmann Archives (page 16)

Edited by Kal Gronvall

Library of Congress Cataloging-in-Publication Data

Italia, Bob, 1955
The Tampa Bay Buccaneers / Bob Italia. p. cm. — (Inside the NFL)
Includes index.
Summary: Covers the history of and personalities connected with the
    team that holds the record for most consecutive losses in the National
    Football League.
ISBN 1-56239-529-7
1. Tampa Bay Buccaneers (Football team)—Juvenile literature. [1. Tampa
    Bay Buccaneers (Football team) 2. Football—History.] I. Title. II. Series:
    Italia, Bob, 1955- Inside the NFL.
GV956.T35I83   1996
796.332'64'0975965—dc20   95-36979
                                                              CIP
                                                               AC

CONTENTS

A Losing Tradition

More than any other National Football League (NFL) franchise, the Tampa Bay Buccaneers are associated with losing. Since they joined the league in 1976, the Bucs have managed to make the playoffs only once. They hold the league record for most consecutive losses, and have had double-digit losing seasons for 12 years in a row.

John McKay coached the Buccaneers for more than four years.

It is not difficult to pinpoint the reasons for Tampa's futility. They have not done well in drafting players. In the Bucs entire history, only a handful of players could be considered stars—players such as defensive lineman Lee Roy Selmon, quarterback Doug Williams, and running backs James Wilder and Reggie Cobb.

Another reason for Tampa's troubles has been the coaching. Only John McKay survived as head coach for more than four years. Those who have followed rarely lasted more than a year.

The future does not look bright for the Buccaneers. A lack of star players remains their downfall. But coach Sam Wyche has come from a winning tradition in Cincinnati. He has been to the playoffs and the Super Bowl, and knows how to build a winning team. If he gets the support he needs, he just may turn the Bucs from perennial losers into consistent winners.

Running back James Wilder
outruns the Cleveland defense.

John McKay
and the Selmons

In 1976, the Tampa Bay Buccaneers played their first season. Their head coach, John McKay, was one of the most successful college football coaches in history while at the University of Southern California (USC). The USC Trojans won nine conference championships, five Rose Bowls, and four national championships.

McKay had a lot of rookies and new players. He knew it would take some time before his team would work together as a unit, and fans needed to be patient. The wins, he hoped, would eventually come. His first objective was to improve a little bit every game.

From day one, Tampa decided to build their new team around strong defensive players. The Bucs used their first pick in the 1976 draft to take Oklahoma University defensive end Lee Roy Selmon.

Selmon grew up on a 40-acre farm near Eufaula, Oklahoma. He and his brother Dewey were the two youngest children in the family. But they were big for their age.

When Lee Roy and Dewey entered high school, each were six feet tall and weighed two hundred pounds. Lee Roy and Dewey Selmon eventually enrolled at Oklahoma and played football. In their four-year college career, Oklahoma lost only two games, and won the national championship in 1975.

That same year, Lee Roy Selmon was named the nation's top college defensive lineman. Lee Roy was chosen first in the draft by Tampa, which used its second-round choice to take Dewey, a linebacker.

Opposite page:
Defensive standouts Lee Roy
(left) and Dewey Selmon.

**Dewey Selmon goes to the air to stop
Los Angeles Rams John Cappelletti.**

Lee Roy Selmon was six-feet three-inches tall and weighed 255
pounds. Though his size was average, he was quick and strong—and
almost impossible to block. Lee Roy quickly became one of the top
NFL linemen, and made the Pro Bowl several times.

Despite the Selmons, Tampa did not play well. In McKay's first
season, the Bucs went 0-14—the only team in modern NFL history to
lose every game in a season.

In 1977, the losing ways did not change as Tampa lost its first 12
games. But in their thirteenth game, the Bucs beat the New Orleans
Saints 33-14. The following week, Tampa Bay won in front of the
home folks for the first time, defeating the St. Louis Cardinals 17-7. It
seemed McKay's patience was starting to pay off. But if the Bucs
wanted to be competitive, they needed solid play from their
quarterback position. So McKay set his sights on a quarterback in the
next college draft.

Doug Williams

Tampa Bay had the second choice in the 1978 college draft. McKay used it to select quarterback Doug Williams from Grambling College in Louisiana.

Williams was six-feet four-inches tall and weighed 215 pounds. He could throw the ball 80 yards in the air. Williams had great potential coming out of high school. He had size, ability, and courage. He would get smashed to the turf over and over, but he'd always get up and play well.

Williams had his doubters because of his race. Over the course of NFL history, there had been few black quarterbacks.

But Williams was not concerned. He knew he had the talent to be successful. "Race has nothing to do with what I can and cannot do," he said. "I feel I'm a solid pro quarterback who will get better with experience. And whether I'm green, black, purple, or yellow, the only thing that counts is my performance out on the field. I feel confident that when people come to see me perform, they will leave knowing I gave them everything I had."

In 1978, Williams played well enough to lead his team to a 5-11 record. But Williams was not satisfied. He knew that he and his team could do much better. He was not content to prove that he could play professional football. He wanted to prove that Tampa could win championships.

Division Champs

In 1979, Tampa shocked the NFL when it won the National Football Conference Central Division title with a 10-6 record. In only four years, McKay had produced a division champion. And in only his second year, Williams had led his team to the playoffs. The defense was the real star. Led by Lee Roy Selmon, the defense gave up the fewest yards and the fewest points in the entire NFL. The Bucs' defense also featured tackle Randy Crowder and two outstanding linebackers—David Lewis and Richard Wood.

Coach John McKay with quarterback Doug Williams.

In the first round of the playoffs, the Bucs faced the Philadelphia Eagles. Tampa jumped out to a 17-7 lead. The defense protected the lead, and the Bucs hung on for a 24-17 win. Incredibly, Tampa had made it to the NFC championship game— and a shot at the Super Bowl.

The game against the Los Angeles Rams in Tampa figured to be a defensive struggle—and it was. The Buccaneers did not allow the Rams to score a touchdown.

But Tampa could not produce any offense either. Los Angeles kicked three field goals and won 9-0. Despite the loss, hopes remained high for the following season.

Opposite page:
Quarterback Doug Williams.

Back to Reality

However, Tampa Bay stumbled in 1980, finishing 5-10-1. In 1981, they got back on track and won the Central Division with a 9-7 record. But in the playoffs, the Dallas Cowboys beat Tampa Bay 38-0 in the first round. Tampa made the playoffs in 1982, but Dallas once again knocked them out in the first round, 30-17.

The following year, Tampa began a long stretch of losing seasons when they finished with a 2-14 record. Before the season, Williams signed with the Oklahoma Outlaws of the new United States Football League (USFL). His leadership was missed, and the Bucs would never be the same.

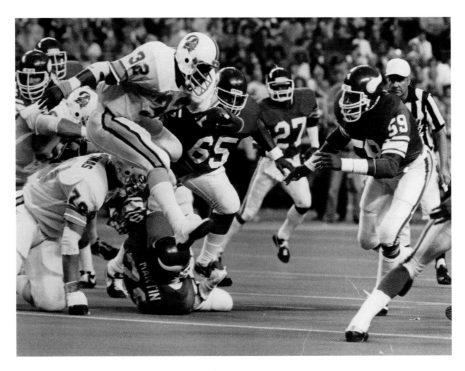

Running back James Wilder leaps over Minnesota Vikings Doug Martin.

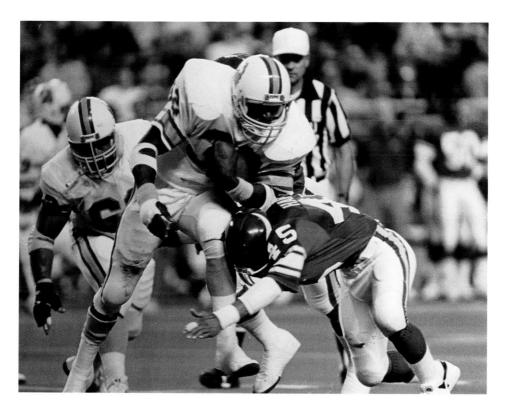

**Wilder quickly became one of the
top running backs in the NFL.**

But in that disastrous season, Tampa found their next star: running
back James Wilder. At six-feet three-inches tall and 225 pounds,
Wilder was a powerful runner who was difficult to tackle. He had
joined the team in 1981 as a backup, and by 1982, he had made the
starting lineup.

Wilder led the team in rushing in 1983 even though he played
most of the year with a rib injury. The following year, Wilder set an
NFL record for most carries in a season with 407. He also rumbled
for 1,544 yards—a team record—and caught 85 passes for 685 yards.

But Wilder could not carry the Bucs on his strong legs. With
Williams gone, the passing game faltered. And so did the team.

When the 1984 season ended, McKay decided to retire. He did not have the energy to rebuild the Bucs again. But new coach Leeman Bennett expected Tampa to contend for the NFC Central Division right away. "Man for man, Tampa Bay has the talent to win it all," he said at the start of the 1985 season. "But this is the NFL. None of the other teams in the league are going to hand us anything. We're going to have to take it, earn it."

Despite Bennett's determination, Tampa Bay finished with the worst record in the NFL in 1985 and 1986. Bennett did not survive.

Having finished so low in the standings, Tampa earned the first pick in the 1986 and 1987 college draft. At least they could look forward to some quality players joining the team. But even having the top draft picks did not guarantee success.

In 1986, Tampa chose Auburn University running back Bo Jackson. However, Jackson decided to play pro baseball with the Kansas City Royals. In 1987, new coach Ray Perkins chose a quarterback who played college football at the University of Miami. Experts labeled him a can't-miss prospect. His name was Vinny Testaverde.

Miami University quarterback Vinny Testaverde tries to avoid an Oklahoma defender.

Vinny

During his college career, Testaverde had led the Miami Hurricanes to a 21-3 combined record in 1985 and 1986. But each year, Miami failed to win the national championship.

Critics said Testaverde could not handle pressure and doubted he could be an effective NFL quarterback. But Perkins didn't listen to them. The Bucs agreed to pay Testaverde $8.2 million over six years—one of the highest salaries in the NFL. To help Testaverde develop his skills, the team hired University of Miami quarterback coach Marc Trestman.

Testaverde impressed the Bucs with his ability and his effort. He worked from eight a.m. to five p.m. five or six days a week. Soon, Testaverde was ready to play in the NFL.

Vinny Testaverde and his parents with NFL commissioner Pete Rozelle at the 1987 college draft.

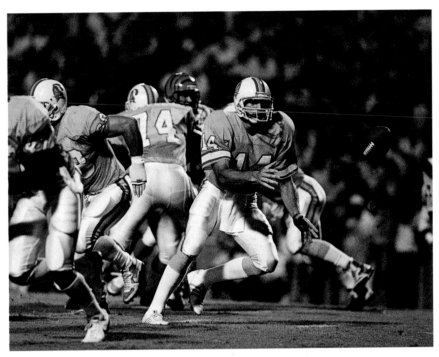

Testaverde was frustrated by his performance, but eventually things started to come together.

At the beginning of the 1987 season, Perkins wasn't sure whether to start Testaverde or Steve DeBerg.

Perkins finally decided on Testaverde, but he struggled throughout his rookie season, throwing many interceptions. But just when it seemed Perkins was about to give up on his young quarterback, Testaverde would have a great game. Against a tough New Orleans defense in 1987, Testaverde threw for 486 yards—one of the top passing performances in league history. Still, the Bucs lost the game, which gave the critics more reasons to doubt Testaverde's leadership ability.

Testaverde was frustrated, but he didn't give up. In 1989, Testaverde began to play better, and so did his team. He threw fewer interceptions and, with the help of wide receivers Bruce Hill and Mark Carrier, began to develop a potent passing attack.

The Bucs' defense was improving as well. They allowed fewer points, and rookie linebacker Broderick Thomas was emerging as a star.

Though Tampa did not finish with a winning season, they beat some quality teams. The Bucs defeated the Packers in Green Bay and kept the Packers out of the playoffs. They seemed to be turning the corner.

A 3-1 start in 1990 fueled hopes for the Bucs first winning season since 1982. But a six-game losing streak brought those dreams crashing down and cost Perkins his job. Perkins' ouster came after the team finally broke the losing streak.

Testaverde was still inconsistent. Much was expected from running backs Gary Anderson and Reggie Cobb, but the ground game still sputtered. A bright spot was the play of free-agent cornerback Wayne Haddix, who made the Pro Bowl. Overall, the Bucs were next-to-last in offense, and next-to-last in defense. Their 6-10 record was not impressive either.

Things only got worse in 1991 for new head coach Richard Williamson. The Buccaneers were bad from start to finish and ended the season with a 3-13 record. The offense only scored 199 points as Testaverde had another poor season. Cobb came on in the second half of the season, and rookie wide receiver Lawrence Dawsey led Tampa in receiving. The defense had difficulty creating turnovers and coming up with the big play. Linebacker Broderick Thomas was the lone bright spot. Sam Wyche came over from Cincinnati at the end of the season to replace Williamson.

Tampa Bay
Buccaneers

10   20   40

Doug Williams leads Tampa to the division title in 1979.

Tampa

Bucca

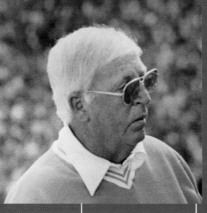

John McKay becomes the Bucs first head coach in 1976.

40

Lee Roy (left) Dewey Selmon join the team in 1976.

20   10

4

James Wilder sets a team
rushing record in 1984.

a Bay

neers

Mark Carrier makes it to
the Pro Bowl in 1989.

40   30

Vinny Testaverde signs
with Tampa in 1987.

Sam Wyche

In 1992, Wyche and the Bucs started 3-1. But then they lost 10 of their last 12 games and finished 5-11. Testaverde's interception problems returned. Reggie Cobb rushed for 1,058 yards with 9 touchdowns, and Dawsey had 58 catches. But the defense still struggled. The Bucs finished twenty-first in team defense and could not stop the pass, even though cornerback Ricky Reynolds was one of the league's best defenders. Rookie linemen Santana Dotson and Mark Wheeler showed great promise. But veterans Thomas and Keith McCants did not play well.

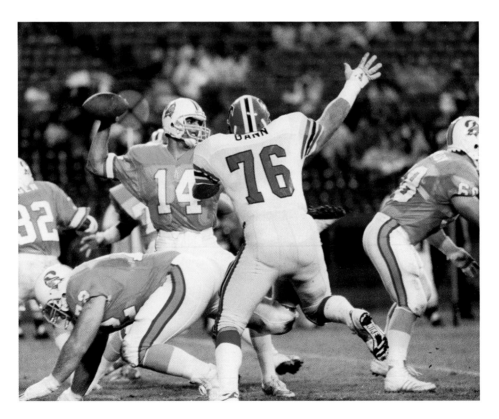

Testaverde looks for a receiver against the Atlanta Falcons.

In 1992, Reggie Cobb rushed for 1,058 yards and scored 9 touchdowns.

The misery continued in 1993. Having owned the league's worst record over the past 11 years, Tampa had their 11th consecutive season with double-digit losses and a 5-11 record. The Bucs started the season losing 7 of their first 9 games by 15 points or more. But then in the last seven games, the Bucs won three times. Quarterback Craig Erickson and wide receiver Courtney Hawkins played well. And the defense, which had allowed an average of 362 yards in the first 9 games, tightened to only 283 yards the final 7 weeks.

Erickson threw 21 interceptions but became the team's first 3,000-yard passer since 1989 and played well down the stretch. Middle linebacker Hardy Nickerson, a free-agent signee, led the Bucs with a team-record 214 tackles.

It did not look like Tampa fans should have any optimism when the 1994 season started. The Bucs lost 21-9 to the Bears in the season opener. The following week, Tampa surprised the Indianapolis Colts 24-10. But by Week 4, Tampa was 1-3 after a 30-3 loss to the Packers. The Bucs gave up 306 yards and 3 touchdowns in the air. Packer quarterback Brett Favre completed 15 of 16 passes in the second half.

Just when the Tampa fans were ready to pack it in for the season, Tampa beat the Lions convincingly 24-14. Vernon Turner returned a punt 80 yards for a touchdown in the first quarter. It was the first kick return for a touchdown in Tampa's 19-year history. The Bucs also scored a touchdown after safety Rogerick Green blocked another Detroit punt, which was recovered at the Lions' 2 yard line.

A Week 8 loss to the San Francisco 49ers dropped the Bucs to 2-5. San Francisco running back Ricky Watters rushed for 103 yards and scored 2 touchdowns as Tampa lost 41-16. The defense also allowed 49ers quarterback Steve Young to hit 20 of 26 passes. If the Bucs wanted to win games, the defense had to improve.

Opposite page:
Craig Erickson became the
starting quarterback in 1993.

Wide receiver Mark Carrier is surrounded by Viking defenders.

But the following week in Tampa, the Minnesota Vikings blitzed the Bucs 36-13. Tampa turned the ball over five times. The turnovers led to 20 Vikings points.

Tampa's record fell to 2-8 by Week 11. The Detroit Lions gained revenge when they turned their star running back Barry Sanders loose for a 14-9 win. Sanders rushed for a team-record 237 yards on only 26 carries. He also set up the decisive touchdown with a 69-yard run. Tampa's rookie Errict Rhett ran for 112 yards in a losing effort.

A Week 13 contest in Minnesota against the first-place Vikings looked to be an impossible challenge for Tampa. But the Bucs took advantage of a dropped punt to surprise the Vikings 20-17 in overtime and snap their six-game losing streak.

The Bucs won the game on Michael Husted's 22-yard field goal, one play after center Ed Brady fell on Eric Guliford's muffed punt on the Minnesota 4-yard line.

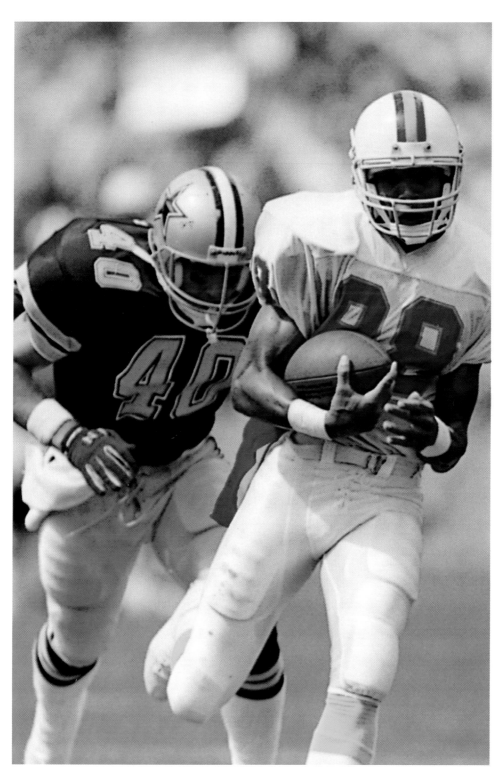

Carrier outruns a Dallas defender after catching a pass.

**Sam Wyche discusses strategy with
his quarterback on the sidelines.**

Tampa led throughout the game until Viking quarterback Warren Moon fired a 40-yard touchdown pass to Qadry Ismail and a 2-point conversion pass to Cris Carter to tie the score at 17-17 with 1:27 left in regulation. The Bucs followed that improbable win with a 26-21 victory over the Washington Redskins. But it was Week 14, and Tampa's record was 4-9. The playoffs were not in their future.

Playing for pride, the Bucs won their third consecutive game in Week 15, a 24-14 win over the Los Angeles Rams. Tampa followed that win with a 17-14 victory over the Redskins. Their fourth win in a row boosted their record to 6-9. Even though the Bucs lost to the Packers 34-19 in the final game of the season, the team's recent success had them feeling positive about themselves and their future.

Rising from the Depths

B ut what does the future hold for the Tampa Bay Buccaneers? Their 6-10 record in 1994 was their 12th-consecutive double-digit losing season. Tampa lacked star players, the defense was weak, and Craig Erickson was still too new and inconsistent to lead his team to a winning record.

Tampa has been in the NFL too long to blame their woes on lack of time. They need sound draft choices, wise free-agent signing, good coaching, and leadership from veteran players if they hope to lift themselves from the depths of the NFC Central. Should they improve in these areas, Tampa may finally shed its losing tradition and become a competitive franchise.

Errict Rhett.

GLOSSARY

ALL-PRO—A player who is voted to the Pro Bowl.

BACKFIELD—Players whose position is behind the line of scrimmage.

CORNERBACK—Either of two defensive halfbacks stationed a short distance behind the linebackers and relatively near the sidelines.

DEFENSIVE END—A defensive player who plays on the end of the line and often next to the defensive tackle.

DEFENSIVE TACKLE—A defensive player who plays on the line and between the guard and end.

ELIGIBLE—A player who is qualified to be voted into the Hall of Fame.

END ZONE—The area on either end of a football field where players score touchdowns.

EXTRA POINT—The additional one-point score added after a player makes a touchdown. Teams earn extra points if the placekicker boots the ball through the uprights of the goalpost, or if an offensive player crosses the goal line with the football before being tackled.

FIELD GOAL—A three-point score awarded when a placekicker boots the ball through the uprights of the goalpost.

FULLBACK—An offensive player who often lines up farthest behind the front line.

FUMBLE—When a player loses control of the football.

GUARD—An offensive lineman who plays between the tackles and center.

GROUND GAME—The running game.

HALFBACK—An offensive player whose position is behind the line of scrimmage.

HALFTIME—The time period between the second and third quarters of a football game.

INTERCEPTION—When a defensive player catches a pass from an offensive player.

KICK RETURNER—An offensive player who returns kickoffs.

LINEBACKER—A defensive player whose position is behind the line of scrimmage.

LINEMAN—An offensive or defensive player who plays on the line of scrimmage.

PASS—To throw the ball.

PASS RECEIVER—An offensive player who runs pass routes and catches passes.

PLACEKICKER—An offensive player who kicks extra points and field goals. The placekicker also kicks the ball from a tee to the opponent after his team has scored.

PLAYOFFS—The postseason games played amongst the division winners and wild card teams which determines the Super Bowl champion.

PRO BOWL—The postseason All-Star game which showcases the NFL's best players.

PUNT—To kick the ball to the opponent.

QUARTER—One of four 15-minute time periods that makes up a football game.

QUARTERBACK—The backfield player who usually calls the signals for the plays.

REGULAR SEASON—The games played after the preseason and before the playoffs.

ROOKIE—A first-year player.

RUNNING BACK—A backfield player who usually runs with the ball.

RUSH—To run with the football.

SACK—To tackle the quarterback behind the line of scrimmage.

SAFETY—A defensive back who plays behind the linemen and linebackers. Also, two points awarded for tackling an offensive player in his own end zone when he's carrying the ball.

SPECIAL TEAMS—Squads of football players that perform special tasks (for example, kickoff team and punt-return team).

SPONSOR—A person or company that finances a football team.

SUPER BOWL—The NFL championship game played between the AFC champion and the NFC champion.

T FORMATION—An offensive formation in which the fullback lines up behind the center and quarterback with one halfback stationed on each side of the fullback.

TACKLE—An offensive or defensive lineman who plays between the ends and the guards.

TAILBACK—The offensive back farthest from the line of scrimmage.

TIGHT END—An offensive lineman who is stationed next to the tackles, and who usually blocks or catches passes.

TOUCHDOWN—When one team crosses the goal line of the other team's end zone. A touchdown is worth six points.

TURNOVER—To turn the ball over to an opponent either by a fumble, an interception, or on downs.

UNDERDOG—The team that is picked to lose the game.

WIDE RECEIVER—An offensive player who is stationed relatively close to the sidelines and who usually catches passes.

WILD CARD—A team that makes the playoffs without winning its division.

ZONE PASS DEFENSE—A pass defense method where defensive backs defend a certain area of the playing field rather than individual pass receivers.

INDEX